A GIFT FOR:

_____

FROM:

_____

Hallmark

Copyright © 2017 Hallmark Licensing, LLC

Published by Hallmark Gift Books,
a division of Hallmark Cards, Inc.,
Kansas City, MO 64141
Visit us on the Web at Hallmark.com.

Editorial Director: Delia Berrigan
Editor: Kim Schworm Acosta
Art Director: Chris Opheim
Designer: Brian Pilachowski
Production Designer: Dan Horton
Contributing Writers: Jeannie Hund, Keion
Jackson, Sarah Magill, Elle McKinney, Courtney
Taylor, Amy Trowbridge-Yates, Melvina Young

ISBN: 978-1-63059-758-0
BOK1090

Made in China

Be Soulful, Be True

UPLIFTING WORDS FOR THE JOURNEY
from 30 Years of Mahogany

Mahogany began in 1987 as a sixteen-card test for Hallmark Cards. Was there a need to bring forth what is most authentic, beloved, and valued about Black culture? To own, celebrate, and express it?

"Absolutely, yes!" was the resounding response. And, of course, we've been celebrating *us* ever since.

As a tribute to our thirtieth anniversary, we've gathered beloved and new Mahogany writing at its authentic, affirming, and uplifting best. This book is both a praise song and a love letter . . . our collective testimony to the power of words to strengthen our spirits and our most meaningful relationships—because we know the need to keep us connected in love, spirit, family, and history remains as strong as ever.

Thanks to all of you who helped us pass that first test and the many that followed. It is our deepest hope that thirty years into the future and beyond, Mahogany will continue empowering you to fully express what is SOULFUL, TRUE, YOU.

Contents

Remember

Who You Are

YOU ARE A

miracle . . .

FROM YOUR *smile* TO *your soul.*

We've always
been told
that it's not what
you're called . . .

it's what you
answer to.

That's more true now than ever.

So please remember this:
You need only answer to things
that make you feel beautiful,
things that tell you you're strong,
and words that call out your
purpose and reassure you of
how much you are needed.

You only need listen to voices of love.

EXPAND

FIT

STEP

GROW

LIVE

AND BECOME

NTO YOUR OWN SPIRIT,

NTO YOUR OWN SKIN,

NTO YOUR OWN STRENGTH,

NTO YOUR OWN FUTURE,

YOUR OWN BLACKNESS,

YOUR TRUE, SOULFUL SELF.

You can *travel* all of Africa

without leaving your room.

Gaze in the mirror

to *journey* there.

March through its

hot sands and golden waters

just by *loving*

who you are.

EXACTLY the shade,

EXACTLY the size,

EXACTLY the way,

EXACTLY the wise,

EXACTLY the person,

EXACTLY the prize

the world needs now.

You are here.

You are *Black*.

You are full of

life and *light*.

You are *rising*.

You are *standing*

You are *singing*.

You are *heard*.

You are *lifted up*.

You are *beautiful*.

You are *you*.

Keep doin' you.

Live the

Dream

19

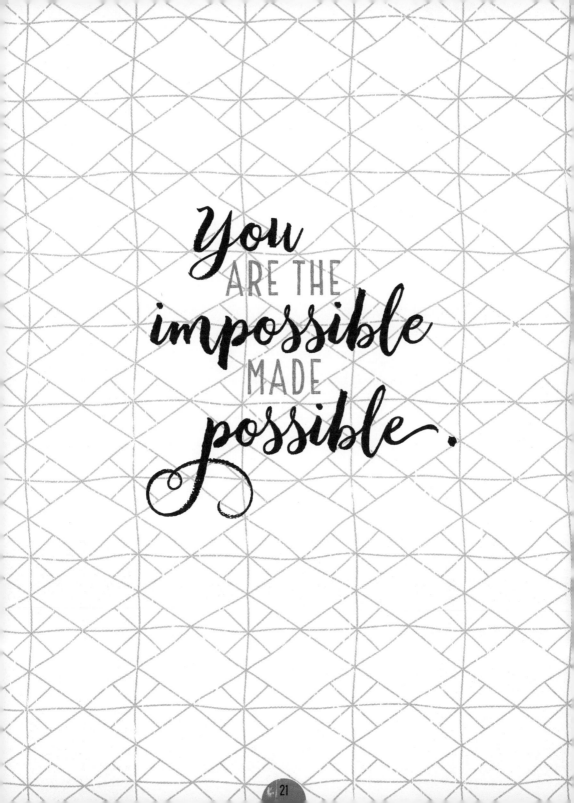

You
ARE THE
impossible
MADE
possible.

Some *dreams*

are *dreamed*

a long, long time . . .

passed down

from *heart*

to *heart,*

generation

to *generation.*

Some *dreams*

get *held high,*

carried along

like a torch,

going *farther* with

each step . . .

'til one day

they become

reality.

We come with *pride* in who we are . . .

with *boldness* in our souls

and majesty in our melanin.

We come with *love* in our hearts

and hope like a blazing fire

that can never be put out.

We come with *history* and *traditions*

that give us our very essence.

We come with *stories* of struggle

and tales of triumph.

But most of all,

we come with *pride*.

AMAZING
DEMANDING
ENORMOUS
UNDAUNTED
REMARKABLE
INSPIRING
ASTONISHING
MIRACULOUS . .

HE PHASES YOU GO THROUGH.

HE TRIALS YOU FACE.

HE HOPE YOU ARE GIVEN.

OUR PURPOSE, YOUR PACE.

LL THAT YOU'RE LEARNING.

HE DREAMS THAT SURVIVE.

OW YOU GROW STRONGER.

OOK AT YOU THRIVE.

Even before you were born,

your name was

"*Freedom*"

and your status

highly blessed.

For the ones who came before—

the ones who handed down the *strength*

and the *wisdom* necessary for

this generation to make it in this world,

the ones who *prayed* and waited up,

the ones who *taught* us to

speak our *truth* no matter what,

the ones who never gave up

and made sure we didn't either—

let us be *thankful.*

UNBOSSED and UNBOTHERED,
UNSHAKEABLE and UNBREAKABLE,
UNDETERRED and UNSTOPPABLE,

32

our CULTURE,

our TRADITION,

our PEOPLE.

YOU.

Feel Love,

34

Give Love

We have arms wide enough to reach,

minds sharp enough to teach,

talent that makes us stars,

courage to heal old scars,

voices that set new trends,

laughter that never ends,

*love strong enough
to be hope for humanity.*

"Sugar" BY ANY OTHER

NAME IS JUST AS *sweet.*

LOVE WITH
fierceness.
LOVE WITH
courage.
LOVE WITH
all your might.

BECAUSE

love

STILL WORKS.

Love makes us *strong.*

Love makes us *proud.*

Love makes us *humble,* too.

Love makes us

more than our pain,

more than our mistakes,

more than our circumstances.

Love *teaches* us.

Love *saves* us.

Love *gives* us hope.

Love *moves* us forward.

Love *holds* us . . .

together.

SOMETIMES *our* hearts

NOW BETTER THAN WE DO.

Big hugs.
Compassion.
Lots of love.
Pass it on.

Black love is a force of nature.

Like rain transforms the desert—

its coarse sands washed new and

softened by the storm—

life springs forth at its beckoning,

a charred and barren landscape forever altered.

Black love is lush.

Black love thrives

in the most unforgiving environments.

Black love is an oasis.

Love
calls you
by your
full name.
♡

SOMETIMES ALL
YOU NEED
IS SOMEBODY

to hug
the stress
away.

Know Your

Strength

You do things in your own unique way.

Keep doing them.

You say things that the world needs to hear.

Keep saying them.

You have dreams that you can make come true.

Keep dreaming them.

Keep going in the direction of your heart.

Slay.
Your
way.

If you can look up,

you can stand up.

If you can stand up,

You can walk.

If you can walk,

You can run.

If you can run,

You will fly.

COMPASSION IS *power.* STAY *powerful.*

keep the faith

break the rules

work it out

play it cool

talk it proud

make it real

laugh and *cry*

hope and *heal*

IF THEY CAN'T HANDLE
your shine,

THEY'RE NOT WORTH
your time.

When you carry yourself

with confidence,

when you speak

your unapologetic truth,

when you apply yourself

with masterful grace,

you are being Black.

You are being

brilliant.

You are being

bold.

You are being

you.

WALK A WALK THAT SAYS,

"I've got this."

Get Up, Get Over

and Get Through

WHEN LIFE
GIVES YOU
lemons,
MAKE
SWEET POTATO PIE.

THROW THEM LEMONS *away.*

YOU DON'T NEED THAT MESS.

People say, "This, too, *shall pass,*"

because it's true.

All the craziness? *It'll pass.*

All the worry? *It'll pass.*

All the nonsense that's going on?

Believe it or not . . . *it'll pass.*

Until then, your *strength* will get you through.

Your *determination* will get you through.

Because unlike all the bad stuff,

those things are *here to stay.*

Nothing CAN BLOCK your blessing.

79

If we must fight,

let's fight for *kindness*,

compassion,

and *healing*.

Let's fight for *inclusivity*,

understanding,

and *generosity* of spirit.

Let's fight for

being fearlessly *hopeful*.

Let's fight for being more *forgiving*.

Let's fight for *love*.

Let's fight for *us*.

When pain comes,

let's *welcome* it long enough

for it to *teach* and *guide*

and *remind us*

we're real and raw,

but also *resilient.*

Then let us send it packing

with a *kick in the behind.*

We have *dreamed*

worlds of *impossibilities*

into the realm of the *possible.*

We've made *ways out* of "no way,"

done *more* with less,

and come from *further* behind

to *reach* our goals ahead.

On the forces of *love* and *faith,*

we *overcome.*

When life knocks you down,

do a smooth floor pose like,

"Cool cool, meant to do that."

LET YOUR
WORRIES
pass
LIKE
clouds.

LET YOUR
GRATITUDE
shine
LIKE THE
sun.

Live
FOR THE
CHANCE TO
live again
TOMORROW.

Claim Your

Joy

Feed the soul

(and go for seconds).

Make room for *sunshine,*

positivity, and *grace.*

Meet every challenge

with a *smile* upon your face.

Laugh off the drama,

dancing as you go along.

Revel in *richness,*

living *happy, proud,*

and *strong.*

Armed with *fierceness*,

jazzed with *grace*,

adorned with **courage**,

and *worthy of*

endless happiness.

Every day

IS A

blessing.

Especially
THIS ONE.

Ain't no shine

like the sun.

Ain't no cool

like the wind.

Ain't no tool

like the mind.

Ain't no joy

like mine.

Make
today
foolishness
free.

Rejoice with the *knowledge*

that every *hope* you spark,

every *kindness* you share,

and every *prayer* you speak

is building a *dream,*

promised to *you.*

Look for miracles.

HINT: THEY'RE
everywhere.

If you enjoyed this book
or it has touched your life in some way,
we'd love to hear from you.

Please write a review at Hallmark.com,
e-mail us at booknotes@hallmark.com,
or send your comments to:

Hallmark Book Feedback
P.O. Box 419034
Mail Drop 100
Kansas City, MO 64141